80/20 RULE

Remove the Friction From Your Life and Become a Better Athlete

HARVIE HERRINGTON

CKBooks

You can contact the author at harvieherrington.com.

ISBN: 978-1-949085-15-0 (print),
          978-1-949085-17-4 (ebook)

Cover design by Noah ~ instagram.com/noarex

CKBooks Publishing
P.O. Box 214
New Glarus, WI 53574
ckbookspublishing.com

The Power of Posture

I want you to imagine this: It's a crucial moment in the game and you make a mistake. You get your quarterback hit. You make a mistake and you drop the ball. You make a mistake and you don't hit the three-pointer. You make a mistake and you strike out. You hit the ground, you break your bat, you bend over, you yell at yourself. You are showing your frustration. There're two things happening now. In your mind you have become frustrated, and in your mind you've started to fall apart. You are getting angrier and angrier at yourself for making a mistake. All of that frustration is building up inside you, so much so that you can't see clearly, you can't hear clearly. That frustration energy is building up clouds and smoke so thick you can't clear your head. That's the first side, your side.

Then there's the other part, the worst part. You have a person like me, your opponent, standing on the other side of the field or on the other side of the court watching you, licking his chops, thinking, *I've got you. All I've gotta do is go harder. You're almost done. I'm about to own your (bleep)*. Showing your frustration is giving your opponent confidence and energy you do not want them to have.

Consider this, what if I look across and instead of seeing your frustration, I see you looking at me, staring into my eyes. Your breathing is perfect, you're calm, just standing there with your hands on your hips waiting for the next play to start. (What does that tell your opponent?) I call that POSTURE. There's nothing more powerful than watching an opponent who has posture. Swagger. Whatever you want to call it.

I remember in the days of Michael Jordan; he had this walk about him. Posture. Even when he missed a shot. Posture. Tom Brady has a walk. Posture. Think about the athlete that you look up to and respect. I bet they have Posture.

I always remind my athletes, never let them see you down. Never bend over. Learn to breathe properly. If you can do that, you can bring yourself back to what I call the beginning. To start over, clear your mind, to remove the clouds. But if you can't, you've lost. I want you to practice good posture. I want you to walk with your head up. I want you to focus on your breathing. Breathe in through your nose and out of your mouth. Some people look at it as cockiness. It's not cockiness. It's posture. It's belief in yourself. It's having no doubt in your abilities, knowing you might get beat but you'll be back on the very next play. Ready to play again. **Posture**

Table of Contents

Acknowledgment

It is with sincere gratitude and a fondess one feels only towards a dear friend that I wish to express my thanks to Lisa Lemons. Everyone needs a team surrounding them to be successful. None of us can achieve success alone. Lisa spent endless hours on the phone with me over countless days helping me put my message together. She has been a Godsend to me. Thank you, Lisa, for your continued help and friendship. I'm so excited to have you on our team. Lives are going to be inspired because of our work.

I've never met this man, yet I can say he has been one of the most influential men in my life. His books and CDs have helped me maneuver my way through life with a lot less friction. I would like to personally thank Dr Robert A. Rohm of Personality Insights. When I read his book *DISC Personality and Positive Personality Profiles* back in college, it was an eye-opening moment for me. It was so powerful that I made a decision to study the information and use it in every aspect of my life. It's taught me about me, why I do, say, and react to people the way that I do. I use it daily with my wife and our children. Now I travel the country sharing this information to educators and our youth. The coolest part is, I get to see the same light bulb turn on that lit up in me so many years ago. I know you'll read this book someday Dr Rohm, especially chapter two. Thank you. Please tell Tiger I said hello.

Mick Snyder, Ken Meuir, Bill Barz, Randy Ball, Bill Wilt, Art Heage, Kelly Sears, David Taylor, Max Kreps, and Charlie Cox. These men may not know it but they were very influential in my athletic career. Without their belief in me and words of encouragement, you would not be reading this book.

What is the Secret to Success?
(Write down your thoughts)

_____

_____

_____

_____

_____

_____

_____

_____

_____

_____

_____

_____

_____

Let's go find out together.

There is a loftier ambition than merely to stand high in the world. It is to stoop down and lift mankind a little higher.

~ Henry Van Dyke

Introduction

Who am I? I feel like you need to understand who I am, and what I've done in my life to understand my desire to write this book, and for you to have the desire to read this book all the way through. I want you to understand my motivation and why I believe I am qualified to write this book.

I was just a kid in grade school when I heard my mother tell a story about this amazing high school football player. The cool thing about it was, it was my dad. Unfortunately, I didn't have him in my life, so I wasn't able to ask him about what I was hearing. I heard the same story several times of how great a football player he was. So I set it in my mind to become a great high school football player, like my dad. It became my driving force.

In seventh grade I started lifting weights in the

kitchen. I would do bench and military presses using 2 chairs to lay on. I did dips on the corners of the kitchen counter. I had no idea what I was doing, but I was working for something (a goal). I wanted to be a great high school football player, like my dad.

My freshman year in high school we had so many players, they had 3 football teams, an A, B, and a C team. I was selected to be on the C team as an offensive lineman. I had no idea how to play football. I rarely even watched games on television. I wasn't a very athletic kid, truthfully. I was short, over weight and dumpy. I was always one of the last kids to ever get picked for anything. I was that kid on the playground who didn't really participate in any athletic activities. But the one thing I can tell you, I knew I was going to play football my freshman year. It was my dream and that dream was more powerful than I could have ever known. That's what I share with students when I speak at schools, how powerful their dreams can be.

Here's what my dream did for me: it took me from the C team to the A team within three weeks. My sophomore year it pulled me to become a starting defensive tackle. By my senior year of high school, I became a leader, one of the captains on our team.

My dream got me a high school diploma and from there I was told I could go on to college and play football! I had never dreamed of football beyond high school. I mentioned the word "pulled" earlier. My dream had begun to pull me. I had no idea at the time this was happening. I just wanted to keep playing football. So I went to community college and played for two years.

After my freshman year in community college, I began to hear about moving on. I was told I could earn a full-ride scholarship to a 4-year university. I kept my head down and worked harder. At the end of my sophomore year, I received seven scholarship offers. With some deep thought and a little luck, I picked the right school (Western Illinois University) and played there for 2 years. I was chosen as captain my senior year by my peers. Here's the crazy part, I still really didn't know how to play my position! Don't get me wrong, I had a great defensive line coach (Bill Wilt). He toughened me up and taught me how to deal with physical pain, but he never taught me how to play my position. He was one of the first adult males in my life that I could look up to as a man.

At the end of my junior year at WIU, I received a letter from the Cleveland Browns. That began to put a burn in my soul. There was a possibility that an NFL team wanted me to play for them. This made me work harder in the weight room, sometimes 4 or 5 hours a day. At that time, we had no strength coach, so I lifted as hard as I could, keeping my mind on the prize.

I got an agent right after we finished up my senior year. He was told by two NFL teams they would draft me in the late rounds. On draft day I received a call from the Washington Redskins late in the 6th round. They said I was next on their board and they were going to take me, but nothing ever happened. It was a very sad night. Thank goodness I hadn't invited people over so I only had to deal with my disappointment. Could you imagine receiving that call, and the last thing you heard them say was, "We are calling your agent and taking you next." I never heard from the Browns. They were the team that showed the most interest leading up to the draft. As fate would have it, I went 2 days later as a free agent. I was picked up by the Indianapolis Colts. It's a great story. They flew me in and I had to work out alone in front of all their coaches. You want to talk about nervous! They signed me that day and I flew home to prepare for rookie camp. From this little, short, overweight, four-eyed fat kid in grade school to an Indianapolis Colt: I was going to be an NFL football player! Now that's the power of a dream!

Weeks later I got cut from the team. I hurt my back in practice and it was so severe I could barely move. They ran tests, took me to several doctors and I was told I needed to stay off of it and rest. I was no longer of any value to the team, and they sent me home. It was one of the darkest days of my life.

But my story didn't end there. I thought it was over until I walked back into the gym. The smells and memories of all that hard work re-lit the fire. After my back healed, I got up and started training again, even though I realized I probably wasn't going to get another shot in the NFL. I still wanted to play football. At that time Arena Football was very popular, so I signed with a team in Des Moines, Iowa.

I played Arena Football for 4 years. I got one more shot in the NFL when the Bears invited me in to do a workout with a group of guys. I kicked butt that morning and they signed me on the spot! Long story short, I ended up having 2 knee surgeries during my time with the Bears. It took me 2 years to recover from those 2 surgeries, but I did. I went back one more time and played Arena Football. At the end of that season I had reconstructive shoulder surgery. I was 32 at that point and the ride was over. I enjoyed every second of it and have no regrets.

Yes, I know, injury prone. The mind was willing but the body wasn't. That didn't matter to me because now I know a lot about dealing with injuries and pain. I've done so much physical rehab that I should have a physical therapist degree. (lol) All the things I've learned in this journey, I'm putting in this book for you. I know it will help you because it is tested information. I've used all of this information to help the athletes I've coached and trained over the years.

My Coaching Journey

I knew I needed to finish my bachelor's degree, so while I was playing Arena Football, I went back to school during the off season and took classes. When I was ready to graduate, I got the dreaded notice I was one credit hour short of graduation. I shared this with my former college coach.

He told me I should go out to the local high school and help them for the rest of the season, which would get me the one hour I needed to graduate.

I went out to help coach high school football. I loved football but had no desire to coach high school football. My very first day with the team was on a Friday night. It was their third week of the season. They lost that game and was 0 and 3. That meant their season was pretty much over. They had to win the rest of their games, 6 of them to be exact, to make the playoffs. I would like to believe that my contribution to those players and coaches, helped them put together the greatest season that school had ever had in its history, before and since. We won all 6 games and made it to the 4th round of the playoffs before we lost. We were one game away from the championship.

At that point I had fallen in love with coaching high school football. Yet I still had no plans on staying, until I met Travis, one of the kids on our team. Travis was a junior, and wanted to play football really bad. However, Travis wasn't very athletic, but he LOVED the game of football. I saw a little of me in him, heck I saw a lot of me in him.

I decided to do everything in my power to help him become a better athlete. I didn't know if he could become a starter but we could at least get him on the field to play. By his senior year he was a starting defensive end and had a great year. Much better than anyone expected. He went into the military and has had a very successful career. I would like to think I played a role in helping him. He learned the 80/20 rule, this is long before I understood what the 80/20 rule really was: **80 percent of the game is mental, 20 percent is physical.**

What I did next was absolutely crazy! I opened a fitness facility to train myself during the off season and our football players. In the matter of a few years it went from training football players to training athletes in all sports. I had girls coming in from softball, volleyball and basketball, and guys from golf, wrestling, track, baseball and other sports. Over the years I had athletes coming from as far as two hours away from other schools to have me train them and I'm not just talking about football players. I even had the pleasure to train Ms. Illinois beauty pageant winners for a few years.

I started learning about training athletes on the mental side as well as the physical side. I read books and went to seminars. I did everything I could to learn how to help these kids become better athletes.

Most athletes go their whole career and never learn these basic principles I've provided in this book. I think back to when I was in seventh grade. If

I had gone up to someone and asked "Can you teach me how to play football?" I would have loved to have them put this book in my hands and say, "Kid, this book is called the 80/20 Rule. It has some great secrets that will help you become a better athlete. Read it, study it, apply it to your life, and watch what it will do for you."

This book will help not only the not-so-athletic person but also the person who's doing ok at their sport. They may not understand that their mentality/mindset may be getting in their way. If it is, it's causing friction and friction in our lives keeps us from performing at the top of our game.

This book is going to teach you about the four personality styles, which one you are, qualities that leaders exemplify, how to remove negative thoughts and create positive ones. I've written it for athletes, coaches, and parents.

Far too many athletes' careers end early because they never went beyond their physical talents. There's a high percentage of athletes who make it to college and the professional ranks just on their talent. They fizzle out way before their time because no one ever passed along some of the basic knowledge needed to reach their full potential.

Am I anybody special? No. Am I anybody great? No. I'm just a person who pursued a dream for thirty-plus years of my life. I have taken this knowledge and put it into this book to help you. I want to help you succeed and create the best you possible.

This isn't a book you can read once. It is a book you have to go back to and pick out certain chapters to read over and over again. It may take a while to sink in, but when it does, you will notice the change. When you do, please help me out by sharing this book with a friend.

Please enjoy.

Nothing so conclusively proves a person's ability to lead others as what they do from day to day to lead themselves.

~ Thomas Jefferson

Chapter 1
Removing Your Friction

Friction

There are some basic questions most athletes ask themselves daily, but they have no idea how to answer them. The problems that created these questions are what create daily **friction**. Let's get busy and answer some of your questions and remove some of your friction.

What is Friction?

This is the crap that gets in your way. It prevents you from becoming successful. Again, the 80/20 Rule. You can be the world's fastest and strongest athlete, which is the 20 percent part of the 80/20 Rule, but it will only take you so far. It's the 80 percent that helps us win titles and championships.

1

How much friction do you carry with you daily that causes you to perform at less than 100 percent?

Your greatest opponent is the person you see every morning in the mirror. Most of us live in daily friction from the moment we wake up until we go to bed. We even carry it into our dreams, which causes restless nights. Just because your eyes are closed does not mean you're at peace. When you have constant friction in your life, it's hard to get things done.

Here are just a few things that cause friction for athletes:

- Listening / focusing
- Talking too much
- Thinking you know more than the coach
- Poor eating and sleeping habits = less energy
- Dating problems
- Doing it for your parents
- Examples: "My dad thinks I can play in the NFL," and "I don't even like football." (It's hard for kids to say no to their parents.)
- Anger issues
- Too much of a people pleaser
- Easily taken advantage of, pushed around, fear of speaking up for yourself.
- Procrastination
- Being too overbearing (a bully)
- Poor time management

Do you struggle with some of these issues?

Imagine if you could get a handle on them or remove them completely. If you can, it will increase your production as a person and as an athlete. You can learn to get out of your own way.

Let's say you worked on being a better listener and learned to focus more. If you are able to listen and focus on what's being taught, you're going to become a better athlete and have a better understanding of your game. I had a big issue with staying focused and when I corrected it, it changed everything.

Can you imagine giving your sport 100 percent of your attention and focus?

Staying focused and remembering plays has always been one of my weakest skills.

I don't have the world's greatest short-term memory. I struggled to remember plays from the huddle to the line of scrimmage, while trying to remember the snap count. In turn, this always made me late off the ball or slow to react. Thank goodness for speed, it made up for that weakness. When I played Arena Football in New Jersey, our team had a connection with the New York Giants psychiatrist. He taught me a 30 second mental memory drill that helped me focus. I took advantage of this right away and noticed an immediate difference. I mastered it in about two weeks. It was a game changer for me.

I instantly got better (Talk about removing a huge amount of friction.) I was never slow off the line again and stopped forgetting the plays. What if I had learned this in high school? WOW!

Less Friction = A Better Athlete.

You get it? Remove the friction, become a better athlete.

Make a list of some of the things that cause friction in your life.

_____

_____

_____

_____

_____

_____

_____

_____

_____

_____

_____

_____

_____

_____

_____

Athletic ability is very important, but it's only 20 percent (physical) of the game, especially by your senior year in high school. The other 80 percent is mental mindset. The Patriots continue to win Super Bowls and beat teams that are far superior to them athletically, but they cannot be beat mentally. They are the most prepared team in the history of sports. That's why they win. **80/20 Rule**

The great players learn how to get out of their own way. They do this by first understanding who they are: why they do, say, think, and react the way they do. They figure out what their strengths and weaknesses are. If you as a player, coach, or parent do not understand this, then you are your greatest enemy, which means you've already lost the game and the season. This is what makes players like Tom Brady perform at such high levels for as long as he has. It can easily be said, the games Tom has lost in the past 15 years were not due to preparation. For the most part it was due to basic mistakes and some athletic ability. (Remember we can't win them all, no matter how prepared and athletic we are.) He's not perfect; no one is or can be. But he pushes his mind and body to get as close to perfection as possible. Here's the greatest part to this: **when you strive for perfection, it begins to rub off on teammates and other coaches.**

You never conquer a mountain. Mountains can't be conquered; you conquer yourself – your hopes, and your fears.

> ~ Jim Whittaker, first American to summit Mt. Everest

Chapter 2
What's your personality type?

How does it affect your game?

I had no idea this had been taught to me back in high school, until I read one of Dr. Robert Rohm's books on *personality profiles*. It was an "aah ha" moment for me. If I had not learned to change my personality, my career would have ended in high school, like most athletes.

These are some basic questions most athletes ask themselves daily, but they have no idea why.

1. Why do I get mad and lose control?
2. Why do I question the coach so much?
3. Why do I push myself harder than others?
4. Why can't I handle constructive criticism from coaches or teammates?

5. Why do I have problems keeping my mouth shut and just listening?
6. Why am I not tough enough?
7. Why do I act like a know it all and doubt others intelligence?

The problems these questions create are what causes your daily **friction**. Let's answer these questions and remove some of your friction.

Which one of these do you struggle with?

_____

_____

_____

In this chapter we're going to discuss the four personality styles. We will cover the good and the bad sides of each personality. Everyone needs to know both their strengths and weaknesses. Some believe you should just focus on your strengths. I personally believe if you don't know your weaknesses, you will constantly step in your own potholes. Potholes slow us down and will eventually destroy us. Your strengths are easy to focus on because they come natural. Cleaning up your weaknesses requires work. The less potholes, the smoother the ride. **80/20 Rule**

Remember the saying "There's no "I" in Team?" This is true, but please understand, when **you** have personal problems, **you** have to fix them. You don't want to be the weak link on your TEAM. Understanding your personality type is a great place to start.

There are four basic personality types or styles. Each type has its own uniqueness and characteristics that separate themselves from the other three. As you read through this material you will find you have a little bit of each personality in you. But one will show itself as more dominate than the others. This chapter is going to explain why you think, feel, act, and react the way you do. After you've figured out yourself, you then can focus on your teammates and coaches. I don't mean you're going to teach them this, instead you're learning how to work with their particular personality. You're going to find yourself saying, "Boy, she's a C personality so I can't cut any corners with her. I have to give her all the facts." This will make you a much better communicator with your teammates.

Outgoing verses Reserved

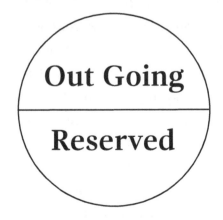

This circle represents the human race. We are going to split the circle into two halves, a top and bottom.

The top half represents people who are **Outgoing**. They love to be around people

The bottom half are people who are **Reserved**. They are not the most social people in the group.

Outgoing People are Optimistic, Positive, Fast-Paced, and have a ton of energy.

Reserved people are Cautious, Concerned, Critical Thinkers, Reluctant, and slow to react.

Task verses People Oriented

This circle is split into a left and right half: Left side is Task and right side is People

Task Oriented People: They love Forms, Functions, Programs, Structure, and Working on projects. I think the word Task explains itself.

People Oriented People: They love Relationships, Sharing, and Friendships. They have a desire to be around people. This one is pretty self-explanatory as well. They are a party waiting to happen.

Now we combine the two circles and come up with the 4 quadrants.
- The "D" quadrant, which is both Outgoing and Task Oriented people.
- The "I" quadrant, which is Outgoing and People Oriented people.
- The "S" quadrant is Reserved and People Oriented.
- The "C" quadrant is Reserved and Task Oriented people.

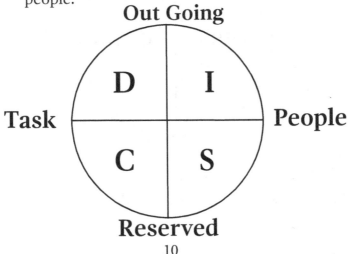

Everyone has a personality type or internal motor. We cannot shut it off or make it go away. It's how we were wired from the beginning. Let's figure out what type of motor you have inside of you.

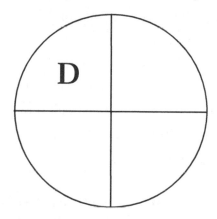

D – Outgoing and Task Oriented
(Muscle Car Motor)

Your "D" personality is like a muscle car (Shelby GT). Midnight black or candy apple red with big tail pipes and drag racing tires on the rear. You were built to dominate life. Your motor is always revved up. Even at rest you're ready to **dominate**. D's tend to walk around with their hands clenched in a ready-to-go position, just in case someone is ready to disagree with them. You don't even realize you do this. You look very cocky and intimidating to the other three personalities.

Let's look at some of the D's characteristics.

D's Personality Characteristics:

Dominant, Demanding, Direct, Commanding, Determined, Insistent, Bossy

D's:

- Are get it done type of people
- Have a hammer
- Their mindset is "I want to win and I will do whatever I need to get it done. If you can't get down with that ... get the heck out of my way."
- Don't have time for small talk
- Are go-getters

D types have to work the hardest to get their motors under control. If you feel you are a D type personality learn to control your motor. Try not to run over everyone in your path. If you can do this, you're on your way.

Strengths of the "D" Type:

- Strong Willed
- Goal Oriented
- Determined
- Deliberate
- Independent
- Self-Confident
- Optimistic
- Straight Forward
- Productive

- Competitive
- Confident
- Quick to Respond
- Big Dreamers

They believe they can win at anything.

A Few Negative Traits (Potholes:)

Rude, Impatient, Pushy, Offensive, Abrasive, a Bully, Cocky, Just downright Nasty

D's Don't Like:

- Rubber lipping (talking without action)
- Being told what to do (if you can't be coached, you won't get better)
- Action with no goals in mind
- People who aren't driven

D's Basic Needs:

They have to be **in-charge**. They need **choices** so they can make the decision. They need to be **Challenged**.

A Little Extra:

- "D" types are very critical of anyone not giving 100 percent
- They are willing to take on tons of responsibilities

- They think anyone who needs a pat on the back is weak minded
- They enjoy Superstardom
- They enjoy being challenged
- They love competition (gotta have it, can't survive without it)

If you feel you are a D Personality, please understand, your teammates may view you according to the negative side of the personality. Please don't think this is ok or something to be proud of. If you do, good luck holding the team together, let alone winning on a consistent basis. You need to work on changing the way they see you. This goes for the coaches as well. People will never give you one hundred percent of themselves if they are intimidated by you or fear you.

This is why certain professional players didn't or can't win championships. I don't want to use names, so stop for a second and think about some of the people you love to watch. If we could interview a few retired players, I bet they could point to something in this book that would have helped them come closer to winning the big game. You can be a high energy pit-bull, growling, dominating, and bullying everyone around you. Yes, that can and will make you look great at times, but isn't it your purpose to win games and championships?

So get your pit-bull under control. Learn to use him to motivate and not intimidate.

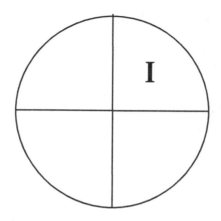

"I" Types – Outgoing and People Oriented
(IndyCar Motor)

"I's" Personality Characteristics:

Inspiring, Imposing, Persuasive, Influencing, Energized

I's:

- High energy, motor is always running revved up and ready to go.
- A party waiting to happen. They are the energy and sometimes the life force of the team.
- Love to talk and can't stand silence. Their skill is the gift of gab, talking, laughing, and enjoying the moment.
- They have a super short attention span and a great ability to shake off a mistake and move on to the next play. (We all need to remember this and commit it to memory.) Don't allow a bad play to ruin a whole day/game.

Strengths of the "I" type:

- Friendly
- Carefree
- Inspiring
- Interchangeable
- Talkative
- Outgoing
- Loves People
- Great Starters
- Personable
- Upbeat
- Positive
- Expressive
- Persuasive
- Spontaneous
- Impulsive

"I's" can be leaders. You just have to remember to keep your energy under control and let it out at the RIGHT moments. Remind yourself every once in a while: God gave me two ears and one mouth. There is a reason for that.

A Few Negative Sides (Potholes):

- Unrealistic
- Likes to gossip
- Illogical
- Always on an Emotional Rollercoaster

- Unfocused
- Short Attention Span
- Loves to play and work at the same time
- Impulsive
- Daydreamers

"I" Types Don't Like:
- Being ignored
- Ridiculed
- Alone time
- Negative tasks
- Being embarrassed

"I's" Basic Needs:

They need popularity, approval, and recognition.

I know you might be thinking; leaders don't need approval. Truth is, they do. We all need it. D's need it as well. Whether it's from a coach, significant other, or parent, we all look for it and need it. Everyone needs to hear, "Job well done."

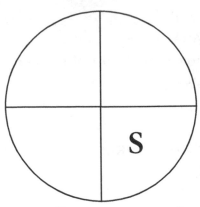

S Type Personality – Reserved and People Oriented (Prius – calm and cool at all times. You can never hear their motor running.)

S Personality Characteristics:

Shy, Sympathetic, Concerned, Sensitive, Helpful, Kind

This is the personality I want you to pay a little extra attention to. There are more S types in the world than any of the other three personalities. Which means there are more S types on your team than the other three personalities. S's are kind, caring, and loving people, which means they may not have the killer instinct they need to win. (But they can train their brain to get it.)

S types are very quiet and even keeled. They never get too excited or fired up. They are natural-born servers. They don't like to be out front and for the most part have no desire to lead. Their desire is to make people around them happy. They just enjoy being a part of the team and going along for the ride. Their goal is to never go against the flow of the traffic. (D's love going against traffic, they welcome it.) S types can become leaders; all they have to do is understand the other 3 personalities, especially the D personality. Learn to change your personality sometimes to meet the situation. I had to raise my D personality on every snap of the ball.

If you are not a D personality, you will have to remind yourself to raise your D when you are faced with tough situations. Practice it enough and it becomes a little easier every time. It's ok when you don't succeed at raising your D. It is a very hard battle for an S type. But when you do, I promise, you are going to be so proud of yourself (I'm smiling as I type this) because more than likely you will be sticking up for yourself or someone else. Don't come down on yourself too hard when you fail to raise your D. There will always be more opportunities coming your way.

Strengths of the S Type:
- Supportive
- Servers
- Dependable
- Stable
- Conservative
- Steady
- Shy

- Sweet
- Loving
- Caring
- Loyal
- Easygoing
- Patient
- Quiet
- Calm
- Reserved

A Few Negative Sides (Potholes):

- Easily taken advantage of
- Lack Initiative
- Indecisive
- Don't like change
- Slow Paced
- Resentful
- Easily pushed around
- Can't take a butt chewing

S's Don't Like:

- Surprises
- Being pushed
- Eye contact
- Conflict of any kind

S's Basic Needs:

They need Security and Accountability.

Coaches:

This is the athlete you can't come down on the wrong way. They tend to harbor resentment when you do. It's not their fault; it's the way they are wired.

Players:

As you read this, please do not use this as your excuse. You have to get tougher if you want to get better.

Here's the difference between an S and a D personality. When a D screws up or makes a mistake and a coach or teammate comes down on them, the D can handle it and move on to the next play. An S will take that butt chewing to the grave with them. It's just how they are wired. So we do have to walk a fine line with this personality type.

Coaches/Captains:

*You have to approach an S-type the right way. I call it the **sandwich method**. Complement them first, find something they did good (the top bun). Then critique them (the meat) and always finish with a positive complement (the bottom bun).*

With this being said, if you think you're an S personality, understand, your parents, coaches, and leaders are trying to help you grow, not tear you down. So tighten up, raise your D, and get after it. The real world is not going to give you the sandwich method; it's going to punch you in your mouth and move on.

In any sport or competitive event, you are going to have an opponent across from you. That person's goal is to beat you down. You need to have the same mentality. You have to raise your D to match the intensity of the moment. Some of us have to dig a little deeper than others, but you can do it. (Go back and look at the characteristics of a D.)

There was a moment for me in junior college, on the first day of hitting. I was up against our best offensive lineman. Needless to say, I was a little intimidated. Brian was a beast. He was the strongest guy on our team. The first time he came off the ball, he kicked my butt; that's putting it nicely. I was embarrassed. The coach called for two more guys to step up. Something in me said no, get back up there and get the job done. I said let's go again, and we did! I brought everything I had to the table and we ended in a stalemate, which for me was a moral victory. If I had gone to the back of the line knowing I had not brought my A game (D personality), I would have mentally fought that for a long time. Brian and I battled all year long and we made each other better. It gave me confidence and belief in myself. I will say, from that moment on I knew I could run with the big dogs in college, and I did.

I've been asked by many players, "How do I raise my D personality? How do I get *meaner*?" One of the greatest places to learn how to release, or grow, your

D personality is in the gym. You can find the **BEAST** in the gym. That's where my beast was groomed. Bench press and deadlifting were my lifts. It's just you and the weights. You have to call on all of your power and anger to pull that dead weight off the floor and to push it up off your chest. Will this happen overnight? No. But week after week, attacking those weights/exercises and setting some big goals to achieve, it will happen. Just be PATIENT and work hard.

Another defining moment in my career:

During the winter of my junior year of high school, I was power lifting two days a week with a few of my teammates. One day, while working out, this tall, huge, muscular guy walks into the gym. He was a former NFL player and he was there to work on rehabbing an injury to get back into the NFL. We had been told he would be coming and we were also told to not bother him as he was there to work. So I didn't bother him. But my teammate Tony did! Tony wanted to get this guy to share some of his secrets with us, and he made it his mission to get the guy to take us out to a park and show us some moves.

Tony worked on this guy for weeks, and at first the guy wouldn't even talk to him. But Tony was persistent. In fact, one day the guy yelled at him, "Kid I don't have time for it, please stay away from me and let me get my work done. I am here to train." Again, Tony was very persistent. (I should have learned something from Tony right then.) He stayed after it and eventually the guy said fine. He said he would only do it just this one time, we were to bring our spikes and jerseys to the park on Saturday and he would show us some moves.

Now Tony was a really good friend to me and he asked if he could bring me along as well. The guy said fine, but said again, this was a one-time thing and don't be asking again!

On Saturday morning we got ready, went out to the park and met this guy. It was December, so it was COLD. He starts working with us showing us some great football moves we can use in the game. At the end of about 45 minutes he stops and says, "All right guys, that's it. Don't ask me to do this again. I'm very busy. I took the time to do this to help you out, but don't ask again." Then he looks at Tony and he starts talking to him.

Now I need to stop here and explain; this guy stands 6'3" and as a junior in high school, I also stood 6'3". But this dude was built! Muscles everywhere. So while I could stand eye to eye with him, I was just a frail, skinny high school kid next to him. Tony was not as tall, he had to look up to the guy.

I am standing there listening to this NFL athlete start telling Tony, "You got it man, you got the "it" factor. You are going to get it done! I don't know where you are going to go to college, but with your mentality, you are for sure going to go somewhere."

Tony was a pretty fired up kid, and you could tell he was really excited about the feedback he was receiving. I'm standing off to the side listening to this and thinking he's going to say the same thing to me. He's going to look at me and say, "Dude, you're tall, all you need to do is keep working out and you are going to get it done." But he looks at me, and we are standing there eye to eye and he says, "Harvie, you don't have it. You're not tough enough, you're not mean enough, and you just don't have the "it" factor."

At that moment I didn't know what to say. I felt like I had swallowed an apple and couldn't get any air. I felt like a little whipped pup who had his tail between his legs and just wanted the moment to be over! But I asked him what he meant and why. Again he said, "You just don't have it kid. You aren't tough enough. You'll do ok playing high school ball, but no college is going to pick you because of your mentality. You aren't mentally tough enough."

And again I asked him why? Why I am not tough enough? How do I get tough enough? Show me how to be tough. He said, "You don't want to know kid." I looked at him and I said, "I have GOT TO KNOW!" You see, he didn't know the power of my dream. He didn't know what he said to me wasn't going to stop me. I said he needed to show me how to be tough, and he did!

I will say he went from 60 mph to 1000 mph in a hot second. It was like turning on a light. He grabbed my jersey and he started yelling at me and he pushed me and kept screaming over and over, "YOU DON'T HAVE THIS! YOU DON'T HAVE THIS!" Now he never hurt me, but he was pretty physical pushing me around. I remember he threw me on the ground and jumped on top of me and got up in my face screaming. When someone is yelling and screaming at you like that they are slobbering and spitting all over. By this time I had already started crying. At that point he lifted me up, and just like he turned it on, he turned it off, and he said, "Kid, you just don't have it."

After years of thinking about it, he was right. Maybe he was trying to teach me something at that point. I would like to think he thought he was teaching me something that would make a difference, because honestly it did. That day he planted in me the D-personality, which is what you just read about. He planted that personality, whether he knows it or not. It took me a few years to really groom it, but I did. I got my "it" factor, a.k.a. D personality.

We never saw the guy again after that year. I began the journey to change my personality. I had to work on it. As I said, I had no idea this had been taught to me, but it was. The D personality is what pushed me through college and into professional sports. If I hadn't learned it at the time, I would have never made it, and you wouldn't be reading this book.

I personally feel it's a blessing to be an S personality, because once the whistle blew and the play was over, I had no problem turning off the **Beast**. This is the biggest problem D's face. The **Beast** never shuts off, and that's when they make really big mistakes. They put themselves and the team in bad situations: late hits, talking back, not listening, and on and on....

If you think you are an S type, learn to turn **it** on (the BEAST), because if you don't, you will get passed up and left behind. The D on the other team is waiting to drop the hammer on you.

In closing, I will say to my S sisters and brothers, get out on your playing field and embrace change. Take some risks, get over being embarrassed and worrying about what people say or think about you. They don't care about you anyway. People mainly just care about themselves. Sometimes you just have to say I don't give a ...

S Types remember this:

We tend to live in fear quite often. Here's what FEAR really means. False Evidence Appearing Real. I'm going to leave this just like this. I want you to think about it. Break down each word. False – Evidence – Appearing – Real. If you don't get it, ask your coach or parents to explain it to you. If they can't, email me and I will personally explain it to you.

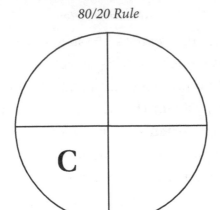

C Type Personality – Reserved and Task Oriented (The Tesla Motor, everything has to be perfect.)

C Personality Characteristics:

Careful, Aware, Diligent, Punctual, Proficient

C's:

- Very knowledgeable and the most structured people on the planet.
- Very orderly, strict, and they follow the rules.
- Perfectionist.
- Very detailed oriented.
- Strategic.

This is Tom Brady, Michael Jordan, Wayne Gretzky, Serena Williams, Tiger Woods, Roger Federer, and all of the greats that live above the clouds.

The great ones all have this personality, whether it's natural or learned. If you are not a C type personality, please learn what a C is and commit it to memory as quickly as possible. Get a complete understanding of this one first. You will never get the full potential out of your body and mind if you don't. There have been thousands of good athletes, but this is what they were missing to become great. Remember this, you can have all the talent in the world but talent can only carry you so far. Talent does not win championships. Understanding this personality alone will change your game. One of the greatest defensive linemen I ever coached (Loren Severs) was probably one of the slowest and least athletic kids on the field his senior year of high school. Yet he was second on the team in tackles because he was a C/S personality. He understood the game, he knew how to play his position, and he was very coachable. If you do not understand the C personality, you're selling yourself short. This is the main key behind the 80 percent of the **80/20 Rule.**

How does a linebacker like Ray Lewis make it to the Pro Bowl in his 15th season? He studies the heck out of the game. He was a quarterback playing linebacker. He started his career as a D/I personality and finished as a C/I personality. Let that sink in.

Strengths of the C Types:

- Calculating
- Competent
- Contemplative
- Careful

- Critical Thinkers
- Consistent
- Correct
- Cautious
- Detailed oriented
- Patient
- Punctual / Early
- Studious (They put in the time studying everything about their game)

If you are going to explain a play to a C personality, you will need to explain the entire play (A to Z), leaving nothing out. You cannot cut corners with this personality. If there is a mistake in your game plan, they'll see it, and point it out to you. C's will question everything you do or say. They are not being disobedient; it's how they are wired.

Coaches:

If you find you are an I or D personality, please focus on this C personality. Let's say you are running a play in practice and the team cannot get it right. Here's what will typically happen. You get frustrated, lose patience and scratch the play or move on. This is especially true, if you are a D or I personality. You have to use your C personality and make sure everyone knows what their job is for that particular play. Be willing to not move on until it's ran perfectly by each player. If you have a play book full of plays that only a few people on your team truly know how to run, that's not going to work. Sure, repetition can get really boring, but that's how championships are won. One of my former players had an opportunity to coach for a school that had won at least 6 state titles in the past 15 or so years. I asked him about practice and what were some of the things he was learning. He said to me, "It's really boring. We run the same play over and over again day after day." I could tell he was bored with it. I just smiled and thought how that coach had won 6 state titles and played in 10 of them. He wears two rings due to all that boring repetition. The head coach of that team is a C personality. They perfected a handful of plays and ran them down your throats. If you do the math on this, here's what it looks like. **Repetition x Repetition x Repetition x Run it until it's perfect = SUCCESS.** Just ask Tom Brady.

Coaches, run your plays until they are perfect and then run them some more. Make sure all players have a complete understanding of what their responsibilities are. I'm speaking from a high school perspective right here. Big time college football is different. They've recruited and given scholarships to the players that know this as well. As a high school coach, I would rather have 8 to 10 plays in my play book I can call and have complete confidence in, knowing ALL of my players on the field know what they are doing. That kind of confidence is what win championships. **80/20 Rule**

Coaches:

Whatever your sport is, whoever is the QB/leader of your team, that person has to learn the qualities of a C personality. Brett Favre would have won at least 4 Super Bowls if he settled down his I personality and learned more about his C personality. (Just my opinion.)

A Few Negative Sides (Potholes):

- Compulsive
- Critical
- Antisocial
- Ask a lot of questions
- Doubtful
- Fearful of something going wrong
- Too detailed
- Cold
- Easily offended because they have to be right
- Don't like change without a plan.

C's Don't Like:

- Being criticized
- Mistakes (theirs or others)
- Ideas without plans
- Mediocrity
- People that don't know what they are talking about

This is what made Tom Brady and Michael Jordan the greatest of all time. They left no stone unturned. Here's the difference between Tom Brady and Brett Favre, another great hall of famer. Brett was a gunslinger (I/D Personality). He had a rocket arm and could move fairly well, so that's how he played the game. From what I've learned about him, the first few years of his pro career, he wasn't very good at reading defenses. He just went out there and played (hence a ton of interceptions). Tom Brady understands his offense better than his coaches. He knew he wasn't fast or mobile, so he needed to know where all the holes were in the defense and became the best pocket passer the game has ever seen. He studied the game (watching film) like no other. He put in his 10,000+ hours and more. (See pages 68 and 69) He took what he had and got the best out of it both physically and mentally. Tom is the GOAT because he uses all four personalities and he's very good at all four of them as well. **The greatest leaders use all four personalities to lead their team.**

C's Basic Needs:

They need the Truth and Excellence.

Free gift to you: So many young people have no idea what profession they want to go into. If this is you, email me. Once you have an idea of which personality you may be, I will send you a list of career professions that fit with each personality (free of charge). www.harvieherrington@gmail.com

The quickest and shortest way to crush whatever victories you have is for you to rest on them.

~ Author Unknown

(This is a reason why some of the greatest champions lose the very next game after they win a really big game or even a championship. It's ok to enjoy the moment, but know when to turn it off. Unless you just won the last game of your career or the season.)

Check google for **free** personality tests. Take one and see what your personality may be. Really study that personality, both the good and the bad sides to it. I also offer personality test and coaching for a nominal fee.

Chapter 3

Negative Thoughts
& How to Remove Them

We all carry around two different mindsets, one on each shoulder. One is positive and the other negative. You have to decide which one you will listen to in every situation you face.

There's a story about a guy who trained racing dogs for a living and won races all over the country. At one particular event, two of his dogs were picked to race one another. When it came time to bet on the race, he had to pick one to bet on. Of course, the one he bet on won the race. He was asked how he knew which one was going to win because they were both very fast. His reply was, "I picked the one with the stronger mindset." We have to do the same thing. We have to feed the right mindset to win. If you fill your mind with negative information, that's exactly what you are going to get back out of life. If you fill it with positive thoughts, then that's what you are going to get back.

Let's go over some negative thoughts and mind-sets people have every day. I call them garbage thoughts. Here are just a few things that run through a negative person's mind on a daily basis. Now keep in mind, I am not saying you have all of these thoughts, but as you read these, some of them will kick you in the gut as they did to me. You will say, "That sure sounds like me."

1. **The Loud Mouth**
   This person yells and has angry outbursts all the time. They can't keep the volume down. When things go wrong, they tend to spout off at the mouth to their teammates and sometimes their coaches. They tend to spew garbage and hateful things all over everyone, which means they have no sense of control over their emotions.

2. **Feelers**
   They accept negative feelings without ever asking themselves why. When the coach gets on them about doing something wrong, they get mad and tend to shut down. As an athlete you have to take your feelings out of the situation and have the ability to see the problem for what it really is. Peyton Manning (NFL Quarterback) was very

good at doing this. If he did something wrong, sure, he would get mad. But what he did after getting mad is what made him great. He went to the sideline and made corrections on his iPad. There was no one better than Peyton at doing this. Most players shut down and lose control of their emotions and thoughts and never truly make it back during that particular game or event. If this is you, you've got work to do. When you get frustrated and your opponent sees it, you will feed that person energy to go harder at you. *Never allow them to see your frustration.*

3. **Know-It-All**
A know-it-all will say, "I know what my problem is. I don't need my coach or my teammates to tell me anything. I know what you're going to say and do to me, so don't waste your time trying to tell me anything. I know what's wrong!" Or something like this, "Coach, I think this is the best way to run this play." This is a great way to get benched. There is a reason the coach has the title of coach. He's the boss. It's his team and you need to listen. If a captain is trying to say something to you or help you, it's your job to zip it and listen. (Bite your tongue until it bleeds if you have to; not in a literal sense.) Remember this, NO ONE likes a know-it-all. You could be seen as a one-upper (I've got a better story than yours) as well. Even

if you are correct on a matter, you have to find the right time to share your opinion.

4. **The Exaggerator**
    This person turns a small simple problem into a disaster. Something that should be an easy fix gets blown out of proportion. I like to call this person Captain Drama. Drama creates cancer and cancer destroys all teams.

5. **Coach Doesn't Like Me**
    You take things very personal (S/C Personality). You can't take constructive criticism. This person is thinking "Coach just doesn't like me." Understand this, the coach is the CEO; his job is to win games. You are just one chess piece on the board. I gained a much better perspective of this once I became a coach. I can truly tell you, if the coach doesn't have you starting or playing, there's a 95 percent chance it has something to do with you. (Great leaders never place the blame on others, even their coaches.) If great players like Michael Jordan and Kobe Bryant were able to take criticism from Coach Phil Jackson, so should you. It's not about whether he likes you or not. You're all there to win games. That is the main objective, especially once you've reached the varsity level and beyond.

Try this. Create two lists: 1. List the things you are good at. 2. List the things you're not good at. Set some goals to improve on both. Start with this question: Am I a likeable person? Then ask your teammates or a friend the same question. Ask them to be honest with you, and let them know it will not affect your friendship. Be prepared for good and bad responses. After that, access the feedback and get to work. Your coach will see the difference and you will get your chance.

6. **The Weather Man a.k.a. Negative Nelly**
You will say, there's a 30 percent chance of rain today versus it's a 70 percent chance of sunshine. Today's going to be a terrible practice because I didn't get to eat a good lunch; I failed my math test; we don't have all the right players to have a great season; one bad series means the rest of the game is going to be bad. You allow one bad thing to ruin your entire day or game! Doesn't this sound pitiful? Yes, it does. I personally feel this is an easy one to change. I call it BPBQ Be Positive or Be Quiet. Put your hand over your mouth if you have to.

7. **Justifier**
"I do things this way because that's how I've always done it. You don't know how hard I've worked, so don't tell me anything. My dad told me this is the

right way to do it. I learned this at last year's summer camp. So, coach, this is the right way to do it." You tend to make excuses for your mistakes instead of owning up to them.

These seven things do not make you a bad person. They are things we've learned along our journey in life. I battle these negative attributes on a daily basis. But the great thing is, I am always on the lookout for them, so I can put a stop to any of them before they ruin my day or my team's day.

Here's how most people attempt to deal with their negative thoughts or emotions:

1. They suppress them.
The old school way is to put it in the closet, suppress your problems. Man up, is what some people will tell you. Well here's what happens when you man up; you become a volcano just waiting to erupt. It's only a matter of time and you're going to explode. Then you've got hot lava (a.k.a. garbage) spewing all over. This is how you get kicked out of the game or off the team. All you've done at this point is become a major distraction, a.k.a. cancer. We do not want to suppress our emotions.

2. Express your emotion verbally.
You let everyone know how you feel and what's

on your mind. This makes everyone as miserable as you are.

If you choose to use either of these two, like most people do, you become a blundering mess and no one is safe or happy around you. You are the cancer.

Let's put out the fire the right way

To get out of your own way you need to put out the fires. You cannot suppress your negative thoughts and emotions, or express them to everyone.

Here are a few things you can do:

1. **Acknowledge the negative emotions**

   Accept that you may have some of these issues and acknowledge them to yourself. Be honest. After all, if you're not, how can you remove them? I was, and I still am, a very pessimistic person (I work on it daily; it's one of my potholes.) But once I acknowledged this about myself and started working on the problem, the dark clouds began to go away. Every time I read a self-help book, it's like a big punch in my face. But I can take it and so can you. The truth hurts, and most of us just refuse to face the truth. I came up with the saying BPBQ; Be Positive or Be Quiet. In other words, if you ain't got nothing good to say, SHUT IT! I learned this from Carla Keller (motivational speaker). I adopted the motto of **BPBQ** and I asked my wife to help me with these pessimistic thoughts and comments. When we're in public and either one of us begin to spew lava, we will say, "Hey, I spoke to Carla today." This will let me know I am headed down lava alley. Now keep in mind, if you ask for help, you have to be willing to accept the help. It's not going to be easy. No one wants to hear someone telling them to check themselves. I've worked on it for years. I didn't become a pessimist overnight and it's not going away overnight. After a few years, I've gotten a pretty good grasp on it. You're still young so it won't take you as long. Please don't get me wrong; I'm still working on it—Along with quite a few other negative traits. Knowing my weaknesses and working on them keeps me from getting in my own way.

2. **Own your emotion**

    Here's what you have to say to yourself: **I Am Responsible (IAR).** This will allow you to put your emotion in check. When you say IAR either out loud or in your head, it will buy you time to make better decisions and get a grip on the situation. It will feel dumb and embarrassing in the beginning. Trust me **BPBQ** and **tGia** (Thank God I'm Alive) still sounds a little weird, but it's my thing and it helps me remove the friction. It will give you control of your thoughts and actions. You have to say it (IAR), even if you know 100 percent you are not in the wrong. I Am Responsible! This is another big game changer. It is the quality of a true leader. **80/20 Rule**

3. Have the ability to see the bigger picture

Scenario: The coach yells at you for making a mistake in practice and you don't think it's your fault. Ask yourself some of these questions before you speak:

 A. What's my goal and what's really important right now at this moment?

 B. If I become negative, how will this affect our TEAM? Will it move us forward or turn us in the wrong direction?

 C. If I argue with my coach, will I lose the trust and respect of my teammates and coaches? These questions will help you when something goes wrong.

4. Retreat

Sometimes you just have to walk away, drop it, and move on. This will give you time to think things over. If you can do this, it keeps you from saying something dumb you cannot get back. Once it's said, it's said, and if it's bad, you're done. No matter how many times you say I'm sorry, you cannot take it back. If it is done at the wrong time and to the wrong person or persons—especially the S personality types—you've caused permanent damage to them as well. **Learn to walkway or remove yourself** when you want to do or say something negative. It protects you and others on the team.

Do not carry your mistakes and bad choices into the next play.

I learned this from my college coach: Have the capability to move on to the next play without carrying the anger with you.

One day in practice a teammate jumped off-sides three times in a row. Coach let him have it. He had him do so many up-downs/burpees that he puked. (Not saying it was right, but he got his point across.) I'm sure my teammate thought he was in the dog house for the rest of the day, but on the very next play, coach spoke to him like nothing had ever happened. I was pretty amazed by that. Coach removed the friction by moving on and not carrying his anger along with him. The ability to move on is very powerful and a hard one to accomplish.

Keeping control of your Emotions

How you respond to bad plays and mistakes says a lot about you and what type of person you truly are.

You're going to make mistakes. You're going to miss a block, miss the shot, allow the goal. It's gonna happen. When it does, what are you going to do about it? Are you going to let it get in your head, replaying the mistake over and over, and allow your emotions to have control over you from that moment on? Or, are you going to try to figure out what went wrong, correct the problem and move on? Chances are there are a lot of games left and a lot more plays (and even more mistakes) for you to make.

An emotional athlete makes mistakes over and over and over again. There is nothing wrong with intensity. There is nothing wrong with energy. There is nothing wrong with excitement. Those are all emotions which should be present when you are playing your sport. Just don't let your negative emotions get out of order.

An offensive lineman's job is to keep the defensive linemen from getting to his quarterback. Most of the time they accomplish their job, but sometimes they give up a sack and they get their quarterback hit, or hurt, or miss a block and get the running back hit or hurt. A great offensive lineman, or any great athlete, always understands there was a mistake somewhere.

Here's what you do after a mistake. Instead of getting mad at yourself and losing your train of thought, you have to first clear your head and realize you made a mistake somewhere and figure out where your mistake is. By understanding where you made the mistake, you increase your chances of not doing it again. To do that you always have to go back to the beginning. A lot of athletes forget that and they don't go back to the beginning, the start; the first step you have to take. That again goes back to the knowledge of what you are doing. If an athlete is out there just playing a game and doesn't have the knowledge and the complete understanding of what he or she is playing, that is a recipe for failure. You need to have complete knowledge of all your responsibilities. Actually, this is the easy part. Knowledge comes thru repetition.

The second part of a mistake is the 80 percent side. The mental side. This is the hard side to correct. Don't get so upset with yourself that you get lost in one mistake when you have so many more plays ahead to make for yourself and for the team. Always come up with a way to clear your mind, a way to breathe out the mistake, go back and look it over in your mind really quick. Sometimes you only have a few seconds to make a correction and get set for the very next play. This goes for all sports; it goes for baseball, wrestling, soccer, basketball, and golf, especially a sport like golf. You know maybe you didn't have your foot turned in or out, maybe you swung too hard, the club face was open, maybe I rocked back off my block. All those little things you have to do to get the perfect play or the perfect move. You just made a mistake, so forgive yourself for that mistake, figure out what it was, and go back and get it done right.

Tom Brady may make an error on the physical side, but you will never see it again. He pops back up and it is like it never happened. It is completely erased from his mind. He never lets the mental side show. It's not easy to gain control over your emotions, but you have to figure out something that works for you. Maybe it's a keyword, maybe it's a wristband snap. Whatever it is, forgive yourself and move on.

I can guarantee you that if you don't forgive yourself, if you allow your emotions to control your game after making a mistake, it's going to be evident. It will be evident to you, to your coach, probably the fans in the stands, but most importantly, to your opponent. That opposing player will then do everything in his or her power to keep you inside your head, to keep you emotional, to keep you making mistake after mistake. Forgive yourself. It was a mistake. Go back to the beginning. Figure out what the steps are and where you went wrong. Correct the steps and move on.

This isn't just for sports. This is life. Even if you are in a job outside of sports, you are going to make mistakes. There are going to be people around you looking for you to mess up; some may even be hoping you will mess up. They are going to do everything in their power to keep you fighting inside your head.

Don't let them! Forgive yourself, make corrections, move on and win!

A leader has to be able to concentrate under difficult conditions — to keep a cool head when everyone around them is losing their mind.
~ Harvie Herrington

Find a security word, something you can say to yourself that will remind you to take a deep breath and get it together, I use my arm rubber band/bracelet, sometimes I have to snap it on my wrist to bring me back.

Chapter 4
Qualities of a Leader

1. **All great leaders have Character.**

   Having character means you have mental and moral qualities, and you believe Truth, Honesty, Respect, Kindness, and Strength are a part of your DNA. This is a person that doesn't waiver and has strong conviction about their beliefs.

2. **Leaders know how to handle FAILURE and how to pull something positive out of it.**

   Never be afraid to fail. Why? Because it's the only way to learn. Just make sure most of your failures occur in practice, where they belong. Please understand, most people are afraid to fail. This will give you an advantage over the average athlete. When you're not afraid to fail, you are more willing to try new things. Practice as much and as hard as you can. The more you learn and correct your mistakes in practice, the less mistakes you're going to make in the game.

3. **Leaders are Goal driven.**
A person without goals has no direction. Without direction you're just walking around in a circle. We all need short, medium, and long-term goals. Short term goals give you small victories. We need the small victories to keep us energized. Why? Because failure shows up a lot more than success. So every small goal/victory you can hit, will keep you moving forward.

4. **Leaders have the ability to look within and see the truth about themselves.**
They know their strengths and weaknesses of both their athletic ability and their mental capacity.

5. **Leaders never lie to themselves or to others.**
It's as simple as that. Make no excuses about telling the truth. The truth stings at times, but it will never hurt you the way a lie will. It's really easy for some people to lie. Lying buys a person quick and fast relief. A lie will always come back to haunt you. Toughen up and make the hard decision and always tell the truth. Truth builds muscles and lies create fat. Muscles make you feel strong and healthy. Fat makes you feel lazy and worthless.

6. **Leaders accept praise but never allow it to go to their head and always give credit.**
   Give credit before you ever give personal praise. Do not toot your own horn. If you become a great leader, enough people will toot it for you.

7. **Leaders are great at serving others.**
   The best leaders are typically the greatest servers. To serve means to always do what is needed to help others, even if it means putting what you want or need second. Your teammates don't care how much you know until they know how much you care about them. If you want to get your team to run through a brick wall **with you,** serve them and show them some love. Never make a person feel like you value them only if they get their job done.

You will always get what you want, if you help others get what they want first.

                                            ~ Zig Ziglar

Coaches: *We should never promote people to a leadership position that did not earn it. If you only have one captain at the beginning of camp, then you only have one captain. Make them earn it.*

8. **Growth is a lifelong process.**
   Just because you've been voted a leader doesn't

mean you've made it. Great leaders are always learning something new via reading, listening to podcasts, or watching YouTube videos. Adopt this motto: **I will be better tomorrow than I am today**.

9. **Lead from where you are.**
    You can lead from the front, middle, and back of the pack. You do not have to be, or need to be, in the front to lead. Don't get bent out of shape because you are not in the front. I was never a head coach for high school football, but I will tell you this, I was as much of a leader of our teams over the years as the head coach was. I put my heart and soul into coaching; I served with everything I had. Here is the truth, people always rally around the true leaders of a team. If you can become the best **YOU**, then you become a true leader. I challenge you to become the **BEST YOU!** Then watch and see what happens. You'll begin to notice things, like how your coach talks to you a little differently. Your teammates ask YOU questions and pay attention when you talk. Here's a little secret. Most of your peers will never read this book. If you study this book and apply these principles to your life, you're not just going to be a great athlete, you're going to be a **great person**. Something in this book is going to change your life. (I know this because all of it changed mine.) I'm a better man because of this information.

10. **Make tough decisions and handle them the correct way.**

When you have to give someone bad news, there is a right and a wrong way to do it. What if your best friend in the world was a teammate, and that person became the biggest cancer on the team? You know they need to change or they have to go. You talked to your coach and she/he told you it was your call. How would you handle this situation? What personality will you need to use and how would you approach this person and where? You have to know all these things before you walk into a situation like this. This is super important, because there are right and wrong ways to handle every tough situation. It will not just affect life on the team, it may also affect life outside of the team for all involved. **Never be afraid of making the hard decision(s) no matter how tough.**

11. **Two ears and one mouth – Listen more than you talk.**

Even as a leader, you have to listen more than you talk. Never get too big for your britches. It's a great way to lose momentum. As a player you may be too close to a situation to see the full spectrum of the problem. Remember, your coaches see things you cannot see. It's their job. Also remember, referees make way more correct calls than they do wrong ones. (Plus, you always want to stay on their good side.)

12. All leaders have great mentors.

Surround yourself with people who are smarter than you, people you want to learn from. Respect them enough that you're willing to listen to them with an open mind. Learn from someone who has walked the path already. Never get caught up in your own mind, thinking you know what's right and wrong. No one is that good. If you don't have any mentors around you, read books on some of the greats.

13. Leaders separate themselves from the team (respect).

If I am your leader, I cannot be your buddy (on the field). This is a tough one. You have to make yourself available to them, yet at the same time keep your distance. It's hard for friends to lead friends; they will expect you to show favor at times. Maybe off the field your relationship can be a little closer. (Set a clear understanding with them; you do not play favorites. You need their respect at all times.) Stop and talk to them at the lunch table but move on. Even if it means you have to sit alone at times. You are a leader and sometimes that can be very lonely.

14. True leaders always earn their position.

Never have your spot given to you. Earn it and you will always have the respect of your teammates. Things that are given to us, we tend not to respect as much. Things that are earned, are cherished. They will follow you if you earn it. They will question you on everything you say and do, if you have not earned your position.

15. Never lead by intimidation.

Putting fear into your team will never work. You have to earn their respect. A leader that leads by intimidation will never have the full support of their team.

16. NEVER PLACE BLAME.

Even if you're 100 percent sure it was the other person's fault, never place blame. Placing blame means you have taken away your opportunity to change or fix the problem. It takes away your power. When you say, "I am responsible, it's my fault; I will make sure it's done right," you keep the power in your hands. Remember if you are the leader, it's your ship, and you have to be the captain at all times.

If it's going to be, it's up to me.

~ Jody Victor

17. **Avoid getting caught up in your title (captain, head coach).**

    Here's what happens to people once they reach their goal: they begin to move backwards. They think they've made it and they will do everything they can do to hold on to that title, instead of continuing to do what they were doing to get there. Don't get caught up with that. It has a tendency to make a person insecure. Don't forget, your team doesn't work for you, they work with you. You are still a **TEAM** working **together** for the common goal: **To WIN!**

18. **Focus on shared goals more than personal goals.**

    The number one goal for the TEAM is to WIN, not YOU reaching your goals. Keep in mind, a team without goals has no direction or common purpose.

19. **Learn how to develop leaders; someday your career will end.**

    You should want to leave your team knowing there are good players coming behind you. It doesn't matter what type of season you had if you don't invest in the future; the program will take a step or two backwards after you are gone. You have to help the coach plant seeds for next year's team. Take it upon yourself to grow more leaders. Find a young whipper snapper and take them under your wing. Share this book with them. Show them some of the things it taught you. That will let them know how you feel about them. (How about that for a plug for my book, lol.)

What are your top 5 qualities you would like to work on?

1. _____
_____
_____

2. _____
_____
_____

3. _____
_____
_____

4. _____
_____
_____

5. _____
_____
_____

Be a measuring stick of quality. Because some people aren't use to an environment where excellence is expected.

~ Unknown Author

(This sucks to say, but so many of us come from such a negative background or environment, that we don't understand or have any idea what excellence looks like. I didn't for a long time.)

Chapter 5
Setting Goals & the Fundamentals

Setting Goals
Before you read this chapter, make a list of the areas in your game you're not satisfied with.

Example questions (write your answers):
- What are you not satisfied with or about yourself as a person?

_____

_____

_____

- What are two things you need to live by to achieve your goals and dreams? Example: Persistence and no procrastination. Improve my leg strength. Foot work needs to be faster, more explosiveness, ability to react without having to think about it.

1. _____

   _____

   _____

2._____

   _____

   _____

- What are the beliefs you need, to create a champions mentality?

   _____

   _____

   _____

   _____

- How will you feel, or will it affect you, if you do not accomplish your goals?

   _____

   _____

   _____

   _____

Goals are a major key to all of life's success.

There was a study done at Yale University in the1950s. They interviewed the graduating class just before they left campus for the last time. They were asked, how many of them had a clear specific set of goals, with a **WRITTEN** plan to achieve them? Less than 3 percent of the people had written down any of their goals. Twenty years later they went back and interviewed this group. The 3 percent were leaps and bounds above the 97 percent who did not have written goals with a plan. The 3 percent who had written down their goals had more wealth than the other 97 percent combined. I know this is not about money. I need you to understand the importance of your **written goals**. You have to get all of your goals on paper, then clean them up and narrow them down to the most important ones; not too many, not too few.

Why have goals?

They inspire you and create the energy and power to make you do what you need to do every day, over and over again. These goals have to be powerful enough to pull you along on the hard dark days. There will be times when you are mentally and physically out of gas. These are the times you may want to give up. Your goals have to be big enough to lift you up on those days. My goal pulled me through some really tough times. While I was in community college my younger brother went to jail on a murder case and was eventually sentenced to 65 years in prison. I had to go through a lot of it with him because he put my name on his confession statement. It was a tough time for our family. I wondered for years how I managed to make it through such hard times, until I began to learn about the power of my Goals and Dreams. It pulled me when I couldn't push myself. It inspired me when I truly needed it. Yours will do the same for you as well. I need you to truly understand the importance of YOUR GOALS.

Why write them down?

Write them down so you can see them and read them daily. Written goals give you something to focus on daily.

Make several copies and keep them with you and read them several times a day. Every day. Especially before practice and bed. **80/20 Rule** (This is another great secret to your success.)

Write down a few goals you have for yourself and your team.

1. _____
_____
_____

2. _____
_____
_____

3. _____
_____
_____

4. _____

_____

_____

Aim for the Eagle, bag the Pheasant so you don't eat Crow.

~ Frank Kessler

For years I heard Frank Kessler, a friend of mine say, "Aim for the eagle, bag the pheasant, so you won't eat crow." It's a nice little saying and all, but what does it really mean? Actually, it can mean a couple of things, depending upon what you personally get out of it. Basically, it's saying give everything you've got to bag that eagle (your goals and dreams), but while you are out hunting (a.k.a. doing the work), you are going to see some pheasants (the things you need in your life to survive). You should capture those pheasants so you have something good to eat if you miss out on the eagle, because if you miss those pheasants, you're going to be stuck eating crow; stuck in a going nowhere job; stuck in the same neighborhood you grew up in, living a life someone else determined for you.

Let's look at my life as an example. My eagle was professional football. My pheasant was a degree and my crow was returning to my old neighborhood and being just another person chasing a paycheck, just getting by.

WHAT'S YOUR WHY?

Why do you want to accomplish these goals?
What's your reason for accomplishing these goals?

You will continue to move in the right direction when there is a target/goal in front of you. A person without goals has no direction. As I've said before, a person with no direction, walks around in a circle. (Remember, I wanted to be a football player like my dad. That's what I worked on. It was my direction. It was my eagle. Every time I hit the eagle, the dream got bigger on its own.) I've learned so much from one simple little dream. You can too if you figure out what your dream is. Your dreams have so much power!

Make sure you know and understand what is going to be required of you to attain your goals. Just writing them down is another form of rubber lipping. **Action is required; you have to put in the work to get to your reward. There is no other way.**

Be careful who you share your dreams with, including family members. People don't mean to but they will unintentionally crush your dreams or put undue pressure on you, by living through you. They believe they're trying to protect you, when actually they are crushing and stagnating your growth. Either keep your goals to yourself or only share them with people that believe in you. They do not have to believe in your dreams. They are your dreams. They just have to believe in you. I wish I could explain this to you better. Most people don't know how to dream, and there are quite a few reasons for this. This is why I speak on the power of a dream, hoping I can start a fire in people. You just have to protect yourself from the dreamless people out there. There are a lot of them!

I want to share a story that just recently happened to me. I was in a gas station and I overheard a couple of the attendants talking. A young girl was talking about her brother. She said he was really good at sports, he was really smart and focused, and that he knows what he wants. He wants to be a professional athlete. She went on to say how she was working to support him, investing her time and money in him because once he turns pro, he is going to take care of the family. He is basically going to save their lives. He would help her out, he would help their mom out, buy them a new home to live in, he was gonna take care of the family. His eagle was professional sports.

Even though he had identified his eagle, his family had not considered what his pheasant was. They were unwilling to consider that he would not get his eagle. This was unfair to the young man as well as the rest of the family. The day will come that he either bags his eagle and becomes a pro athlete, or he won't. At that point his dream and his family's dream is over. It was his dream; it should not be his burden. It is not his responsibility to 'save' his family. It is not his family's dream. Each member of the family should have their own eagle to hunt. They must find the balance between supporting his dream and pressuring him to save the family.

It is inspiring to hear stories of a young athlete that succeeds and is able to support their entire family. There are thousands of young men and women who have that dream. Many of them are from lower income families. They should not play that sport, thinking they will save their family. They need to play that sport thinking, *I am chasing after my dream and I am giving it everything I have.* It's their eagle. It shouldn't be the family's eagle. So again, I say aim for the eagle, bag the pheasant so you do not eat crow.

It also works on the other side. There are kids that grow up in very nice neighborhoods, live in really nice homes, have parents that drive nice cars, and they have nice clothes. They know their parents are rich and they're going to inherit that money. That inheritance becomes their eagle. When you have a life like that, you may not be as motivated to figure out what your own eagle is, or what your pheasants are. That can also destroy a person's life. In life you have to aim for your own eagle. You have to know what it takes to get to your eagle, all the work, all the failing, all the pain and loneliness you have to deal with. It's one heck of a journey, and you must bag every pheasant you can along the way. The money may be gone before it gets to you. You must bag the pheasants.

For most athletes, the eagle is going to college to play sports. Whether its basketball, football, wrestling, track, soccer, it doesn't matter. If you can earn a scholarship, that means getting an education should be just as important as trying to do your best in your sport. There is room for both. You want to be a professional athlete; that is your eagle. What if you don't become a professional athlete? You need to recognize you need a pheasant in life, and that's your degree. If you are a scholarship athlete wanting to play sports in college and you're giving it your best but you know that your best is not good enouph to become a professional athlete, you still have to understand the pheasant is your degree. The pheasant is your trade. It is your safety net.

A Little Deeper Insight

Closed minded people don't realize they are closed minded. Example: Years ago there was a study done on a group of crabs. A professor put them in a really large cage with the top of the cage open. The last two inches at the top of the cage had an electric barrier. There was food placed at the top of the cage for the crabs to eat. Every time they would climb up and get close to the food, they got shocked and would fall back to the floor. This went on day after day. They tried to climb out, over and over again but couldn't take the pain of the electric shock. Over time the crabs stop climbing up to eat and just waited to be fed. No matter how much time went by or how hungry they were getting, they wouldn't climb to the top any more. One day they removed a crab and replaced it with a new one. The new crab decided to climb to the top to get food. The older crabs began to pull it back down. Every time it tried, they would pull it down until it would no longer climb up. As time went by all the old crabs had been replaced with new ones. The electric barrier was removed, but none of them would ever climb out. This is what has happened to a large percentage of the human race. We tell our youth, don't climb up there, don't go and experience all that pain and failure. Stay here and we will be fed in a few days. That's very sad, isn't it? But it's the truth. I want you to be a 3 percenter. Keep climbing and never give up. If you can feel the pull from the crabs in your life, keep your dreams to yourself until you have enough confidence, strength, and power to shout it out to the world. Don't allow anyone to kill your dreams.

Fundamentals

Master the fundamentals of your position. We watch professional athletes, then try to mimic their game so much we have a tendency to skip the fundamentals. Example: In the NBA the 3-point shot has become so popular that kids are now stepping back behind the 3-point line and taking those shots, before they learn how to properly dribble a ball or master all the different ways to make layups. The fundamentals are your foundation. If you do not have a strong foundation, when the storm comes, your house will fall.

There is a great book by Malcolm Gladwell – *Outliers* – that talks about becoming a master of your craft. In a nutshell, it says to master your craft you have to put in over ten thousand hours of work. Hold up! Don't get scared. A master is a professional athlete. Let's do the math. It takes an athlete at least twelve years to become a master. (Four years of high school, four years of college, and four years of playing in the pros, twelve years total. 10,000 hours /12 years = 833 hours a year, divide that by 365 days in a year and it comes out to be about 2.5 hours a day.) This means you have to average about 2.5 hours of training a day, 17.5 hours a week. In four years of high school that's about 3,640 hours. (This can be one of your goals, to practice your craft every day for 2.5 hours.) Don't let this scare you; just remember 2.5 hours on average a day. This is for the person who wants to get the absolute best out of their potential. If there is something inside of you saying, "I want to be the best," I just gave you a working formula.

You might be saying, why in the heck do I need to put in this much work? When you put in this kind of work it's going to give you the confidence you need. Here's what confidence means: You will be ready for everything that comes your way. Very rarely will anything surprise you. When you win, you'll know why, and when you lose, you will also know why.

An unpracticed athlete will always falter when the game is on the line

~ Unknown Author

What are the basic fundamentals of your sport? If you don't know ask your coach. It is important you understand what they are. You need to master them; they are your foundation. (Write them here.)

_____

_____

_____

_____

_____

_____

(Every person is reading this book for their own reasons. If you have no desire to become the best athlete you possibly can become, it's ok. No one should judge you for that. You should always want to be the best you. That's what's important.)

Just a few stories that inspired me along my journey.

Michael Jordan had the flu during a play-off game in the finals.

Story has it, he was running a 102 temp. Here's the difference between him and the people below the clouds. I believe most people will make it through the flu and get their work done, but it will not be their best effort. MJ knew his team needed him to be at his best. He was their leader. Leaders don't just lead when things are going great. He knew if he didn't bring his A game, they could lose. You never want to lose a playoff game. Sure, he had Scottie Pippen, and he was a superstar as well, but he was Michael Jordan, #23, and MJ was a superhero to all. Superheroes always show up. The man dropped 35 points that night, and, of course, they went on to win the series and a championship. Sure, there are some things that will keep you out of the game. However, if you have the mindset of "You're going to have to drag my body off this court," you will always be on the right side of things.

Muhammad Ali Rumble in the Jungle

George Foreman is six foot three inches tall, 260 pounds of raw muscle. He was a tornado and Ali was in his path. Ali was loved by all, but people didn't think he was the greatest anymore. He was past his prime and on his way out. I don't believe anyone, including the people in his camp, truly believed Ali could stop this beast. Ali was different; he wouldn't allow the thought of getting beat by George to enter his mind. Sure, he knew George was stronger and younger, so he came up with a **plan** to beat George, and he shared it with no one but himself. Can you imagine this, sitting there thinking about what it was going to take for him to beat George? You hear a voice say to you "Yes, he's bigger, younger, and stronger than you. Two hundred and sixty pounds of muscle. To beat him you have to let him beat on you until he wears himself out. You've seen the video of him hitting the punching bags. All you have to do is outlast his muscle endurance, because it will go away. It always does." Can you imagine thinking about this, coming up with this as your solution? I'm going to let him beat on me until his muscles wear out; until he has no power left. I'm going to wear him out by letting him beat on me. Say that out loud to yourself. "I'm going to allow one of the strongest and hardest hitting men on the planet to beat on me, until he gets tired!"

Ali went into preparation mode; preparing his mind (**80/20**) to take the beating of a lifetime. It was the greatest fight of all times. It placed Ali above the clouds.

This was all mindset (**80/20**). You've got to have the mindset to believe when no one else does. Have the power to turn off all the outside noise and get the job done. That's what greatness is made of. What will be your Ali moment in your life?

Joe Montana

You're the quarterback and your team has the ball. If you don't go down the field and score, you're going to lose the game and ultimately the Super Bowl. This is the kind of pressure that requires 100 percent of your mental capacity. You begin driving down the field and get a few first downs. The pressure begins to build and your teammates are starting to get nervous. While standing in the huddle you turn to look at the crowd and say "Holy cow that's John Candy (comedian/ movie star) up there." Under that kind of pressure, Montana stopped and enjoyed the moment. Why? Because he had prepared his whole life for moments like that.

Why am I adding this story? Because, the only reason we know about this story is his teammates talked about it. They were in awe of how cool Joe was under so much pressure. They knew their superman was there with them and ready for anything that came their way. Who knows, Joe may have been saying this to keep himself calm.

Are you that cool under pressure? Do you want to be that cool under pressure? It's takes the **80/20** rule.

These two guys are hall of famers but do not live above the clouds.

This story takes place during an NFL playoff game, late in the fourth quarter. His team is winning and all they have to do is stop the offense from scoring. There's only a few seconds left on the clock. This defensive lineman goes down with a knee injury. He gets up and immediately falls back to the turf. He couldn't put any pressure on his knee. He gets up again under his own strength and hops off the field on one leg from the opposite side of the field. He knew if he stayed down, the clock would stop and give the offense a timeout. If a defensive player goes down, it automatically stops the clock. The offense had no timeouts left and he didn't want to give them a freebee. **Bruce Smith** was a warrior on the field. He looked past his pain and showed selflessness. That was all for the team and pure mental toughness. Imagine having this type of mentality. You are so focused on the TEAM winning that it doesn't matter what happens to you. I get fired up just typing this. You've got to be **selfless** not selfish. Learn to look past your wants and needs. Always know what's best for the team.

Every defensive player is always looking for the big hit. Why? Because it feels so dang good. This guy is a true Monster of the midway. He hit a receiver so hard coming across the middle in the end zone, it knocked him out. Instead of getting all hyped up and shouting to the mountain tops, which is what most players do, he immediately dropped to a knee and held the unconscious players' hand until they carried him off the field. I was impressed such a hard-core athlete would do this. Make sure the athlete you love to watch has great character, because if they don't, there is truly nothing worth learning from them. Your character is so important. Do what is right at all times, not just when it is convenient. Yes, you have to have a killer instinct to be a champion, but always show respect and decency to others. That's what **Iron Mike Singletary did.** He went from a D personality to and S personality within seconds. That's what **you** have to do when the time comes.

He was Mr. Irrelevant in the NFL draft, one of the last players to get drafted. The team that drafted him had just signed their starting quarterback to a ten year, one hundred-million-dollar contract. Meaning, they were just filling a spot or looking for a third string quarterback, a.k.a. scout team player. He had one of the worst appearances in the NFL combine; too slow, no strength, just ok footwork, and a mediocre arm. The perfect recipe to not make an NFL team. Now he is the greatest quarterback to ever play the game (19 years and counting). There is too much to talk about when it comes to Tom Brady. No athlete in history has ever performed at such a high level for as long as he has. Tom Brady inspired me to write this book. He exemplifies everything I have written about in this book and so much more. I feel honored to live in the time of these amazing athletes. They have shown the world what it takes to be the best and stay on top for as long as they have. (Michael Jordan, Tom Brady, Tiger Woods, Serena Williams and Roger Federer.) Of course there are others; I just personally feel these athletes live above the clouds. They took it to the highest level possible.

Leadership is a privilege, and with privilege comes responsibility.

~ Sir. Winston Churchill

It can take one positive thought to set you on the path to new change...

When **change** is needed in your life, it should all start with your thoughts. We all need to reset or re-train our thoughts. Even the most positive person has to train their mind.

I have always wanted to know what Tom Brady was thinking in the 3rd quarter of Super Bowl 51 against the Atlanta Falcons. He found his team down 28 to 3 in the 3rd quarter. In the world of football, that's pretty much a done deal; especially on such a huge stage like the Super Bowl. Most of us are not mentally strong enough to come back from being down in such a pivotal moment. This requires strong affirmations. You cannot just start affirming to yourself when you need it most; you need to be prepared for it long before the time comes. Practice affirming to yourself how good you are at your sport. Say to yourself things like: I am the greatest player in the world at my position(s). I've practiced and studied for this moment. I will go back out and complete my passes. I will make the correct choices. I will make the shot. I will catch the pop fly, never miss a note, not be nervous, etc.

Affirmations

Affirmations are used to reprogram our subconscious mind, to encourage us to believe certain things about ourselves. They are used to create the life we want for ourselves. When you repeat an affirmation to yourself, out-loud or in your mind, you begin to retrain your mind to see these affirmations as absolute truth.

Positive affirmations

Positive affirmations are written sentences people use to describe who they want to become and how they want their life circumstances to be.

- I know, accept and am true to myself.
- I believe in, trust and have confidence in myself.
- I eat well, exercise regularly, and get plenty of rest to enjoy good health.
- I learn from my mistakes.

- There is no one better or tougher than me.
- I will work as hard as I can to accomplish my goals.
- No one will **outwork** me today.
- The work I do every day will prepare me for my journey.

There are negative ones as well, but we don't need to talk about those.

How many times a day should you practice your affirmations? I recommend at least three times a day for a minimum of 90 to 120 days; every morning, before bed and once throughout your day. In the beginning you should say (or read) your affirmations more than this; the dedicated one's will.

When starting your affirmations, make sure you are alone.

1. Stand in front of a mirror and look yourself in the eyes.
2. Focus on your breathing, inhale through the nose and out of the mouth.
3. Say your affirmation slowly and clearly.
4. Really focus on the meaning of each word.

Every time you read or listen to an affirmation, it becomes a stronger force in your life.

Read it. Say it. Think it. Believe it and it shall become true.

I affirm to MYSELF, I will be better today than I was yesterday.

Write down a few of your own affirmations:

_____

_____

_____

_____

_____

_____

_____

_____

Focus drill

When I was playing Arena Football out in New Jersey, the team was lucky enough to have full access to the New York Giants facility. We trained there and used all their equipment. The Giants also had a team psychiatrist and one day he happened to pull me aside and ask if I needed help with anything.

I told him my biggest problem was remembering the plays. I would be standing in the huddle, the quarterback would come in and tell us the play and give us the snap count, but somewhere between the quarterback saying "ready break" and getting up to the line of scrimmage, I would forget either the play or the snap count, or both!

If you are an athlete, and you suffer from that type of short-term memory issue, it's hard because it slows you down. If I forgot the snap count, I had to wait until I saw one of my teammates move, rather than listening to the quarterback call the snap count. If I forgot the play, then I had to react by looking at a teammate to see where he went and follow the play that way. *It's a horrible way for any athlete to play a sport.* You are always a few steps behind the play. Luckily, I was a good athlete, and my physical side made up for my mental side. Plus, I thank God for my love of fooball because I didn't allow my memory issue to get in my way. I struggled with it in high school. I struggled with it in college. I struggled with it even in the professional ranks in the beginning. Until the day the psychiatrist asked if I needed help, and he taught me this simple little drill.

He pulled out a pen and said, "Harvie I am going to hold this pen up and I want you to focus on the head of this pen. The head of this pen is blue and I want you to focus on it hard. Then I am going to start the clock and for one minute we aren't going to say anything. I'm just going to hold it, and you are going to focus on it for one minute."

Our minute went by and afterwards he asked me what could I tell him about the pen. I was able to tell him the pen was blue. That was all I could tell him about the pen. But I could also tell him what color shoes he was wearing, the color of his jacket, and also over in the corner was a sign I had read. That was just the way my mind worked. It didn't focus. He then told me I had a really short attention span, but he went on to explain that in sports, as with all things in life, things come in short spurts. Little movements and actions that don't take too long. He said even when you are teaching something, depending on what it is, you're going to teach it in short little teaching segments.

Think about sports. Most sports' plays average about 5 to 15 seconds, with the exception of soccer and wrestling, which are pretty much continual. The average football play is about 10 seconds. It takes about 10 seconds for an at bat (the pitch and the swing), about 30 seconds to hit a golf ball (addressing the ball, and your practice swings), 30 seconds to run down the court, set up your play, and shoot the basketball. Just about any sport, he said, takes about 30 seconds a play, and he was going to teach me to lock in and focus for one minute.

What he had me do next was to focus, really concentrate, on my breathing. Breathing relaxes the mind as you inhale through your nose and exhale through your mouth. He had me take a couple of those breaths. Breathe in through the nose, exhale out through the mouth. Inhale, exhale. Inhale, exhale. Then he brought out his pen again and said to only focus on the pen while continuing to inhale through the nose, exhale out the mouth. I wasn't to let my mind leave that pen for even a moment. We did that for a minute and it worked! I was able to stay focused on that pen!

He told me it was going to take a while to really

train my mind to focus, but I worked on it. I worked on it in my room, and I worked on it in the huddle during practice. When the quarterback would come into the huddle I would start concentrating on my breathing. Breathe in what he's saying and exhale out. Breathe in the play call, exhale out. Breath in the snap count, exhale out. I walked up to the line of scrimmage and when the ball was snapped, I knew the snap count, I knew the play, and I was able to move much quicker, knowing where I was supposed to go. It was amazing! It was really life changing for me.

This technique worked so well for me that I started teaching it to all of my athletes. I had a team one year where so many of the kids really had trouble focusing. I taught them this technique, but I put my own little spin on it. I took a piece of cardboard and drew a huge black circle on it. I can't tell you the circumference of the circle but it was BIG and covered almost the whole piece of cardboard. Every day at the beginning and end of practice, we would do that breathing drill. Over the course of the season, I made that circle smaller and smaller. They got used to concentrating, on focusing. It removed so much friction from that group and allowed us to have a decent year.

There are a lot of athletes that will never be taught this. This would be a great drill for young girls and boys out there with a short attention span, who don't understand why they can't focus. Practice it for a minute. Practice in front of a mirror. Just stand there and focus on something for a minute, breathing in and exhaling out.

You never really get over having a short attention span. I still use this technique today. It's just a part of my life, a part of who I am. But this drill, this technique, has changed my life.

How do you go from good to Great?

This is for the person that may already consider themselves a top-notch athlete on the physical side, the 20 percent side. This makes me think of a young man by the name of Brett, who I coached in my last years of coaching. In order for him to go from good to great, there were extra things he needed to do. He was a phenomenal athlete. He had what coaches call raw talent. During his high school years, he pretty much just played the game on raw talent alone. Our coaches didn't know how to coach him; we just turned him loose and told him to "find the ball." I helped him with a few things, like how to blitz a hole, and he did the rest.

This information is for an athlete like Brett. You need to know everything there is about your sport; you can't just be raw talent. It will carry you pretty far, but there will still be limitations, mental limitations, the 80 percent. You need to fall in love with your sport. Become a sponge. Learn everything you can about your game and your position. If you can do this, the game will slow down. You will feel like everyone around you is playing in slow motion. You hear all the really great players talk about it. I personally experienced that twice in my career.

I know this is repeating what I just said, but you really need to understand this point, *what separates the great ones from everybody else, is understanding their sport better than anyone else.* The Serena Williamses, the great football players, the great soccer players, they all know the ins and outs of their sport better than anyone else.

Let me give you an example of what I mean using football:

If I am a defensive end, I need to know what the tackles next to me are doing, and what the two or three linebackers behind me are doing. That way, I know where all the holes are. I know where everyone is supposed to be. That gives me a better understanding of what the play is and why the coach called it. But, if I'm just playing my position and don't know anything else, it puts me in a box. You never want to play in a box. Trust me; I know what it feels like, I did it for years.

Now, what will this require of you? It will require **everything**. It's going to take 100 percent of you. It will require hours and hours of studying your sport and your position. It will require you coming up with questions, getting them answered and then going back to find more questions. No matter what sport you are playing, you should know at least a little about your teammate's responsibilities for each play. You don't need to know their technique(s), just know what they are supposed to do. Have the ability to see the whole play, not just your part in it; the whole field, not just your position on the field. This is where the extra studying comes in and pays off. If you can do that, put in the extra time studying and really learn your sport, your coaches will talk to you differently. They will know you understand what they're trying to get across to the other players. This is how you EARN a leadership role, even if you did not get picked to be up front. Your knowledge of the game will make you a leader. Just remember, **YOU ARE NOT THE COACH!** Know and understand your personality and do not allow it to get in your way. **80/20 Rule**

The physical side, the 20 percent

Did you know, as an athlete you need at least 10 hours of sleep a day? This is because you recover and grow in your sleep.

Did you know you should be eating about every 3 hours while you are awake?

Are you taking the correct supplements? Do you even need supplements?

How much fluid should you take in on a daily basis as an athlete?

What is your core and why is it so important?

_____

_____

_____

Are you a fast or slow twitch muscle person?

_____

How do you increase your speed?

_____

_____

_____

What are the right drills to improve your lateral movement?

_____

_____

_____

_____

What type of lifts should you focus on for your position, not your sport?

_____

_____

_____

_____

Why is flexibility so important?

_____

_____

_____

_____

Why do you need to ice certain parts of your body after training?

_____

_____

_____

_____

If you are a receiver, how many balls do you need to catch EVERY DAY to have great hands?

_____

If you are a soccer player, what type of cardio training do you need to do in order to have enough stamina to go the whole game?

_____

_____

_____

How many calories do you need to consume daily to keep in peak condition for your sport?

_____

Should you eat before practice, or before a game? How many hours beforehand should you eat? What should you be eating?

_____

_____

_____

_____

Do you have a goal chart of where you want to be with your body throughout the year?

What's the desired weight for your position? How much weight can your body hold and still maintain your speed?

_____

_____

Answer all of the questions in this section, and come up with more questions, on your own. Then get the answers to them.

These are just a few of the questions I came up with on the fly. There are so many more. Remember, this is not for everyone. You can enjoy your sport without having the answers to all of these questions.

Physical perfection in the world of sports is knowing your body and having a complete understanding of it. This includes knowing how your body works, what your body is capable of doing, and what it needs in order to stay at maximum performance. It means knowing every inch of your body. To achieve this, you must be willing to give up everything else in your life at this moment. You are not Tom Brady. He will be 42 years old soon and he's still one of the best QB's in the league. (Unheard of and may never happen again.) He got to where he is because he put in the time and effort to work on making his body better, and studying the heck out of his opponents; figuring out their weak spots.

It is important you understand, the actual playing side of sports is a very short period of time in your life. You can coach as long as you want, but playing is a very short window of time. Just like everyone else, you WILL run out of time. Four years of high school and college will go by really fast. So burn your boat, give it everything you've got and see what you are made of. I promise you will not be disappointed in the outcome.

Burn the Boats

When I work with and speak to athletes, we do a drill called Burn the Boats. Years ago, I read a story about a Spanish Commander Hernan Cortes and his conquest of Mexico back in AD 1519. When their ships arrived and all the men and materials were unloaded, he had his captains go out in the dark of night and burn all of their boats. He turned to his men and said "Look back, I've burned all the boats. Now we have no other options. There will be no retreat. We will either die in battle or win. If we win, we will take their boats and all their gold and return home victorious." Their ability to retreat and return from the way they had come had been removed. No boats meant no safety nets. There was only one option.

Most people give themselves an out. I get it; that's called security. You don't need that kind of security in sports. You can burn your boats and give it everything you've got. You may not win a championship, but you will win in life. The things you will learn about yourself is going to be a game changer for you now and in the future. I often remind my former players, how hard they worked in the weight room and running hills late at night. They were committed to getting better and willing to do whatever it took to get there. Which means they had it inside them to do great things in life. To be special and kick life in the nads if they have to. Sometimes we all need to be reminded of that.

So I am saying to you, burn your boats! Study the heck out of this book. Apply these rules in your life daily. **And believe great things are coming your way!**

In closing

I'm not some great athlete or championship-winning coach. I'm the guy who gave everything I had to my sport. The information I've provided for you are things I've learned along the way. It would have made my career better if I'd have known these things back when I played. Sports saved my life in so many ways. There was no greater love in my life for a very long time.

This is life changing information for any young athlete. There is nothing new to this information. It's been around for a long time; it just got lost along the way, especially in high schools. Now that you have read and studied this information, you have no excuse. I've given you all the information I would have given to my younger self. I am using these rules and principles to raise my children right now. Just like you, they will have to apply them daily or it will not work.

If you didn't skip to the last page to read the conclusion, then this book has served its purpose. There is something in you that has changed from reading this book. I may never get the opportunity to meet you (I would love to come and speak at your school and to all of your athletes and coaches), but I believe in you100 percent. Reach out and say hi. Send me an email. I promise I will respond. As long as it is a positive question or comment.

Great videos to watch. Have a look at my Facebook page:
https://www.facebook.com/coachherrington/
Over the years I've posted quite a few videos on

there. Great footage and information from pro athletes. Great information to view before practice and bed. It will help you get your mind right.

Lord, when I am wrong, make me willing to change; when I am right, make me easy to live with. So strengthen me that the power of my example will far exceed the authority of my rank.

~ Pauline H. Peters

What's the secret to success?

Answer: A person is what they think about and act on every day of their lives with no FEAR of failure.

About the Author

There are all sorts of camps out there to help you get PHYSICALLY better.
This Book is a camp to help you get MENTALLY better. It's going to strengthen the six inches between your ears.

Harvie Herrington developed a dream of playing football early on in life. Inspired by tales of his father's football prowess, he played football all through high school, college, and eventually the NFL and Arena League. He coached high school football for over 18 years and owned and operated his own fitness facility.

After football he took the skills he had been using all of his life, studying and listening to people, and turned his dream into his passion: to help people find their weaknesses and get beyond them. He helps young men and young women to get the most out of their careers and is especially dedicated to those who aren't the fastest, strongest, or most athletic.

Harvie says, "There is no greater feeling than helping someone remove their doubts and reach their top level. It's so rewarding because I was that athlete in high school. It was only my love and passion for my sport that carried me as far as it did."

Today Harvie lives in Iowa and travels the nation speaking to students, athletes, coaches, and teachers. His goal is to share the information he has learned in his life. To help people figure out what is holding them back and inspire them to become their best. Harvie has three children ages 14, 11, and 7. He and his wife use the principles he has shared in this book daily.

Visit Harvie on Facebook:
    facebook.com/harvieherrington
    facebook.com/coachherrington
or Instagram:
    instagram.com/harvieherrington
or go to his website:
    www.harvieherrington.com.
View some of the videos he has posted or leave a message. He promises to respond.

Made in USA - North Chelmsford, MA
1044886_9781949085150
01.17.2020 1208